"A BETTER WAY"

Lawrence R. Mathews J.D., B.B.A.
(Anpu Waset)

1

"There Must Be A Better Way of Doing This!"

www.inspirationalphilosophy.com
lrmathews60@yahoo.com
480-495-3309

Published by Lawrence R. Mathews Opening The Way

Copyright ©2009 Lawrence R. Mathews

Library of Congress Control Number: 2013939679

Book Cover Design by Lawrence R. Mathews
Book Cover Photos by Lawrence R. Mathews

The author is available for lectures and may be reached at the address above.

ISBN: 0-9786346-4-0

"Do Not Allow What You Think or How You Think to LIMIT What You Think or How You Think!"

By: Anpu Waset

"There Must Be A Better Way of Doing This!"

Table of Contents

"There Must Be A Better Way of Doing This!"

Introduction

"A Better Way Is Here!"

Have you ever said the following phrase "there must be a better way of doing this?" You could have been talking about health, relationships or a variety of things when it was said. Wouldn't it be nice to have at your fingertips a step by step roadmap that guides you to discovering a better way of doing whatever you said this about?

This book is composed of various columns that have been published previously in newspapers, magazines or on-line magazines. Typically the columns were written on a monthly basis and were devoted to a specific type of audience. This audience was made up of readers who at one time felt like there was/is a Better Way of doing one or a variety of things. Previous columns are now chapters in this book.

For some, this statement was made about an isolated aspect of their life: for example, their career. However, for most of my audience, the expression was used because of a feeling they had about life itself. These people had reached a point in their lives where they began to question the validity of how life is lived itself and life's purpose. You too are in this club if you have ever said the following: *"There must be more to life than this! There must be a Better Way!"*

"There Must Be A Better Way of Doing This!"

I wrote these columns to assist the reader in discovering **"Better Ways"** of living life and living it more abundantly. Each column presented **"A Better Way"** for the particular topic being discussed that differs in approach and degree from the current practice in that area. Until a person finds that ultimate happiness and contentment (free from pain and sorrow) then a constant search for **"Better Ways"** of handling life and its circumstances must be searched for and then practiced.

The column topics were determined by looking at the most common areas in life where people have had a moment in which they have felt like and stated *"there must be more to life than this!"* Some of the topics included: Male/Female Relationships, Death, Addictions to Emotional States, Politics, and Race in America.

Therefore the columns/chapters in this book are not in sequential order. You can pick any chapter in any order to read, reflect and then meditate on the Better Way presented.

The following method was used when writing each column. The topic being discussed was evaluated by first looking at the current practice/way of being which lead to the statement. This evaluation looked objectively and critically at the thought process in effect which gave rise to the practice.

Then the reader was asked to step outside of his or herself for a moment to look at the current practice. This gives the reader the ability to gaze (or look at) the situation from a distant perspective. This step helps the reader discover the root cause of the underlying thought process. Then a **"Better Way"** of approaching the situation was presented based upon the evaluation that had occurred. The following questions were the center piece of this evaluation and discussion:

1. What is the current idea "driving" the current practice/way of being?
2. Where did the idea come from?
3. Did you make a conscious effort to adopt this idea or was it something you accepted unconsciously?
4. Is the idea true? And finally is it an idea that will stand the test of the time?

A person's practice/way of being in life is a direct reflection upon the ideas they have about life in that area. It is really true that *"so as a man/woman thinketh, so shall she/he be!"* Unfortunately many times men and women do not "think about what we think about!"

Question number four is the most important question to ask yourself. Is the current practice based upon an idea that will stand the test of time? How many ideas of days gone by have been found at a later time to be untrue? People thought that the Wright Brothers were crazy for thinking they could fly. That was a crazy "idea" to many people of the day. But the popular "idea" was not the correct one. Airplane travel is not looked upon as a big deal anymore. We have come a long way from thinking that flying was a crazy "idea."

There are areas in peoples lives in which they adopt practices based upon "ideas" which will not stand the test of time. These ideas unfortunately are unconscious so we do not recognize them. It is these kinds of "ideas" which give rise to the feeling which leads a person to say *there must be more to life than this!"* The discovery of these "ideas" allows us to remove the current practice associated with this idea and allows us to adopt a **"Better Way"** in this area of our life.

Chapter 1

"Am I Addicted To My Emotions?"

I just found out that I might be addicted to my emotions. Until recently I never knew that there was such a thing. But based upon a documentary I saw called "What The Bleep Do I Know," I believe that I might be an addict. The idea presented in the documentary about addictions is much different from the one I had always known. Drug usage, cigarette smoking and alcohol use were the things I was familiar with regarding addictive behavior. The documentary presented the idea that a person is addicted to anything they cannot exercise control over. This new idea made me pause and reflect on the following questions:

1. What if this new idea about addictions is true?

There are many aspects of my personality that I am not in control of. So does this make me an addict to all of them? If this is true, how should this new idea on addictions impact my idea about life and how I live it presently?

Defining an addiction as anything a person cannot control has far reaching implications. Very few people can control their emotional state. Even fewer try. This new definition would mean that a person unable to control him/her self from the "woe is me victim" mentality is addicted to this emotional state. If true, behaviors once considered normal would now suddenly be abnormal.

10

There have been many areas in my life where I was not able to exercise control over an emotional state. One area was my dislike of my father. My father left our family when I was a small child. For most of my life I grew up being very angry at him. I tried to let it go but was never able to do so until he died a few years ago. I never thought about controlling this emotion. No one ever told me I should or could control my feelings regarding my father. But if the documentary was correct, then this was an example of me having an addiction which lasted approximately 35 years of my life!

Initially as I watched the documentary, I said this was "mumbo jumbo" science. I said to myself: "You can't be addicted to an emotion or an emotional state. I'm not addicted to being angry at my father. Addicts have to have a fix. This didn't happen to me." But as I reflected on my own situation, I realized that this did happen to me. It just looked different because it wasn't the typical classification of an addiction that I had known previously.

I was always mad at my father. The anger motivated me to be different from him. When things went wrong I blamed him. Resultantly, I <u>always</u> had a present reason to be angry at him. Everyday I created a reason to get a fix of anger. Even when he was nowhere around.

The documentary indicated that what we call emotional states are actually chemical proteins (peptides) that are regularly released into our blood stream to help the body function. What we identify as an emotional state is actually nothing more than the release of a specific peptide. At the moment of release, these peptides alter our view of reality. Alteration #1 we may call anger. Alteration #2 we may call love and so on. There is a different peptide for every emotional state that we have. It is these peptides that we get addicted to. Our cells become so used to a specific chemical peptide that we <u>constantly</u> create the circumstance for its release. For me this came in the guise of being angry at my father on a regular basis.

I must admit that this information has blown me away. What do I do with this new information? Am I addicted to the emotional states beyond my control? Should I change my idea of what life is and how it is to be lived based upon this new information? If I don't want to be addicted to drugs or alcohol why would I want to be addicted to anything else? What should I do?

In your life, think of emotional states that you may be addicted to. Are there people or circumstances in your life where you create reasons to get "a fix" to have a particular emotional state? Ask yourself these questions to figure out if and where you are addicted to your emotions.

Chapter 2

The Great Tragedy
"Race in Society"

The arrest of Professor Henry Louis Gates Jr. on July 16, 2009, one of the pre-eminent African American scholars at his home in Cambridge, Massachusetts, has long been forgotten as a news story. However reflection on what happened and what this arrest meant regarding race in society is appropriate. Those who remember this situation may recall hearing a variety of commentators and experts on race providing opinions on how the United States of America as a nation can overcome its problems of race in the country.

I noticed that the arrest of Mr. Gates Jr. created a different response from three different groups in the United States. One response came from the African-American community. The second response came from the European-American community. The third response and the group it came from is the subject of this chapter. This response came from a group composed of differing ethnicities within the entire national United States community.

The African-American and European-American groups responded in the usual ways. The former saw is it as more racism while the latter saw it as indicative of a man who would not follow instructions.

13

The third group composed of differing ethnic people saw the arrest as tragic while simultaneously seeing it as a potential step in healing racial issues of the past. They realized that even with the election of an African-American President, as a nation, much work remains to be done in the area of race relations. This group sincerely wanted this event to lead to concrete solutions on how to move beyond this divisive issue.

At the time of the arrest, I initially responded like those in Group one. As an African-American, I was caught up in the "racial" aspect of the issue. Although I am an "inspirational philosopher" in the practice of living life beyond the western societal cultural value system in place currently, I still "identified" with the decades old "us versus them" mentality.

However, after much reflection and thought, I now realize that the most important response actually came from the third group. They realized the importance of moving beyond the issues of race and showed a desire to find solutions to this issue right now. Unfortunately, I did not hear a solution which would solve the problem. That's because one topic was missing from the dialogue.

A solution to the race issue cannot be articulated until we first realize its cause. As a collective community we ALL have one thing in common. We are ALL reacting to the subject of race as seen through the lens of a western societal cultural value system that has consistently produced division and animosity. Living life from this cultural point of view produces the differing views on race in the United States society. Until this cause is addressed and eradicated, no solution will be found.

One way to move beyond the current beliefs about race can be found by choosing to adopt and then practice a different cultural value system that does not produce racial division and animosity. One such cultural system can be found in Ancient African philosophical traditions. The way of living life in these traditions was utilized with success for thousands of years. These cultural systems spread out all over the world and were practiced in similar ways by indigenous people all over the world. These systems did not create division or animosity in terms of race. They did the opposite. They created a mindset which made people receptive and helpful towards others with differing ethnic skin colors. This is why the indigenous people of the lands were helpful and receptive to the European explorers whenever and wherever they arrived.

These traditions were based upon living life less egoistically and more ethically by necessity instead of by feelings and emotional desires, and by living life in accordance with balance, truth, order, justice and righteousness. Life lived in this way, paves the way for people to see the similarities between each other as opposed to the differences.

Given the recent genetic finding that 99.9% of human beings across the globe are alike, mental notions of division based upon race are simply not true. This means that these notions are born from ideas derived from a culture and system of values and not in accordance with truth. If we really want to eradicate racial division and animosity, then adoption of a cultural value system based upon our commonalities should replace the one currently in effect.

Chapter 3

"The Illusion of Pain"

I have yet to meet anyone who consciously likes experiencing emotional heartache and pain. It seems safe to say that the average person would be perfectly all right if they never experienced either of these again. Consider the following. If there was a method which could remove emotional heartache and pain from your life forever, would you consider it?

A person can eliminate these emotions forever. The method is mental and is based on the ideas we have about these emotions and the part they play in our lives.

At an earlier time in life I was introduced to the idea which said that emotional heartache and pain are real. Over time this idea changed into reality and I believed this was true. Mentally, all of a sudden I believed these emotions were a normal part of human life. However this idea is not true. Upon reflection these emotions are something we create based upon our actions. They are self inflicted unconscious creations.

I recall as a small child believing in the idea that I was supposed to grow up with both of my parents. My mother and father divorced when I was about 5 or 6 years old. I don't know where I got the idea that my parents should stay together forever. I was very young so I'm sure no one verbally told me this. Maybe I got the idea from the programs I watched on television. The idea could have come from seeing other families in my neighborhood with two parents in their household. Where I got the idea from now is not important. What is important is the fact that it was mistaken and I believed that it was true. It took most of my life to discover that the belief of having two parents growing up was the cause of much of my emotional heartache and pain.

For much of my life the belief in this mistaken idea caused me to feel like I had been deprived of something. I felt like I had missed out on an important part of life and that I had been abandoned. And at the tender age of 5 or 6, a little boy felt like he had to "grow up" and be the "man" in the family. Needless to say this "grown up" mindset caused me to become reclusive as I began to keep my feelings to myself. I didn't know any better and thought sucking things up and not showing emotions was the "manly" thing to do.

It is now clear to me that this idea was mistaken and not true. There are two reasons for this realization. First, different ideas produce different mental constructs and experiences. For example, a different idea such as "growing up with one parent was just the way it was," or "coming from a single family home gave me just one parent to focus on....." would not have given me a reason for being in pain like I was under the mistaken idea. Additionally in life, no one is promised a rose garden. The idea that life is supposed to be the way we think it ought to be is not based in reality. Nothing happens according to a self scripted plan. Life is what it is and unfolds in that way.

With this realization comes freedom because the tendency to emotionally attach ourselves to mistaken ideas is stopped. We can then respond to life events and situations with balance and poise. Actions performed can be done in the moment free from the desire to achieve a particular result. Emotions then become servants of this person instead of his/her master. Living in this way produces a deep level of contentment.

I now understand that pain is caused from the belief in ideas that are mistaken. I believed that I was supposed to have a family structure the way I thought it should be. That gave me a reason to feel bad when it did not happen. Had my idea been different, my feelings about my circumstance would have differed as well. I now see that my entire concept of pain was nothing more than an illusion that I unconsciously created. Now instead of creating pain against my best self interest, I can do the opposite and create joy, peace, contentment, and happiness. Creations that allow me to have the type of life I say I want. A life filled with joy, peace and unconditional love!

Chapter 4

"Religion Can Unify"

Generally speaking, those people believing in the existence of God regardless of their religious practice share the common following view. They believe that there is only one God. Despite the differences in how these groups worship this "One God," they are united in the belief of this oneness. This united belief seems to be a reason for uniting groups who practice religion differently. However, this is not the case. In fact the opposite is true. Religion today does not unite people. Religion today divides them. Quite often the only unity found in religion is between those who practice and worship in the exact same way.

This is an interesting phenomenon given the meaning and definition of the word itself. The word "religion" comes from the Latin "relegare" which uses the roots "re" which means "back" and "ligon" which means "to hold, to link, to bind." When originally coined it meant to link or bind the individual soul back to its original source: God.

Religion was originally considered to be a set or series of practices that bind or link the individual soul or consciousness to God or Universal Consciousness. So any practice which provides this link would be a religious practice. Somehow over time the definition and original meaning of religion gave way to the present notions of what religion means. Without an understanding of the

20

original meaning of the word, it became easy to fight and bicker over perceived differences between groups. This has been unfortunate as the perceived differences are nothing more than expressions based upon differences in culture and language. While some religions judged, ridiculed, and even allowed the outright killing of people who practiced differently, the underlying belief in the existence of one God never changed in any of these groups.

Religion can unify. Binding or linking the individual soul back to GOD is unification in the highest degree. When practiced in the way it was originally coined, religion can unify all groups and all people. Not just those who practice in the exact same way and manner. When religion does not unify all groups and people, then consideration should be given to whether that practice is being done correctly or whether the practice itself is authentic.

Religious unity can be practiced by having people "bind" themselves around the similarities of different forms of religious expression as opposed to fighting over the differences. With objective and reasoned consideration of the similarities between each group, this process does not have to be difficult.

However unity of this type can only occur when people allow themselves to be open to considering other peoples' practices free from judgment. Mark Twain, the famous author and humorist, made an interesting point when he said "*The easy confidence with which I know another man's religion is folly teaches me to suspect that my own is also."*

Freedom from this type of judgmental thought is the first step which will allow religion to unify different groups. The common shared belief in the existence of one God is far more important than how this belief is practiced. Unification around this similarity will allow religion to be practiced in a way that unifies instead of divides.

Chapter 5

"Death of A Loved One"

On June 25, 2009 the world witnessed the unexpected passing of the King of Pop Michael Jackson. Each year around this time people from across the globe reflect, mourn and are saddened by his death. Although death is assured at the time of birth, little thought or reflection is given to the idea of death until it occurs. At that point people typically gloss over the idea and look at it from the perspective that they have suffered a loss. But does death mean that there has been a loss? Where did this idea about death come from in the first place? Most importantly is the idea true?

There is another idea about death not often considered by the majority population of the western thinking world. That is the idea which says that there is no such thing as death. The premise of this idea is that nothing actually dies. Things make transitions. Although there are many who would outwardly not ever consider such an idea, these same people often unconsciously act in accordance with this point of view.

For example, the major western religions believe in the concept of a heaven and hell. Both Christians of many denominations and Muslims of many sects believe in this concept. Inherent in this belief is the idea that each person's soul/spirit will either live *forever* in heaven or burn *forever* in hell. Therefore both Christians and Muslims believe that the soul/spirit of a person is eternal. Something which lives *forever* must be eternal since it does not die. Although people from these groups may *say* they do not believe in transitions, their actual *belief* is much different.

If it is true that the soul of a person is eternal, then the current idea of what constitutes life and death is badly mistaken. The current idea can be expressed in the following way. "We are human beings having intermittent spiritual experiences." This idea contradicts the opposing view which can be stated in the following way. "We are spiritual beings having an intermittent human experience."

Where does the current idea about death come from in the first place? It is my understanding that it is an idea born from the western thinking world community approximately 2500 years ago. Those of African, Mexican, Asian and Native American descent have unconsciously adopted this view. The premise of this idea is that human life is the reflection of a body which moves, talks, and interacts in the world without any outside force. In this view the skin of a person constitutes the body and this body, by itself, is "alive."

The fact that the skin is actually an organ no different than the heart, liver or kidneys is forgotten. Resultantly this premise fails because the skin organ cannot be "alive" anymore than the heart or kidney organs can be. It is this western thinking world idea about death which is the cause of heartache, sadness, disappointment and pain when death of a loved one happens.

24

The Soul (The True Essence of a Person)

There is a "Better Way" to view death that will free us from the current sadness and sense of loss experienced when it occurs. This is the idea that says that there is an essence which "enlivens" the organs making up the body. For now I will call this essence "soul stuff." This "soul stuff" is the true essence of a person. Every living thing has this "soul stuff" because it is the absence of this "soul stuff" that constitutes death. When this "soul stuff" is present, the person is said to be alive. When this "soul stuff" leaves the body, that person is said to have died. Everything that is alive in creation has this essence.

But as stated earlier, this "soul stuff" cannot die. It is eternal. It was eternal before it "enlivened" the body and continues to be after it departs. The body of Michael Jackson or any person during their funeral is nothing more than a shell. But the body has always been nothing more than a shell. We have adopted the western world idea that the moving body constitutes that which we call life.

Therefore there is nothing to mourn. There is no reason to grieve or be saddened. Nothing has been lost. In fact there is much to be content with. Our stay on this plane was a temporary one from its beginning. There is no such thing as death. Consequently our ideas about life can evolve. Instead of mourning the death of a loved one, this new idea allows us to rejoice in the transition being made and simultaneously eliminate the need to suffer heartache

25

and pain.

Remember it is the soul of a person that is actually alive not the body. Acceptance of this idea about what constitutes life will free us from the misery of sadness and pain currently experienced by many when the death of a loved one occurs.

Chapter 6

"Politics or Polit-"tricks!"

Politics is the way that democracy is exercised in the United States of America. It is the expression of the words articulated by Thomas Jefferson in the Declaration of Independence that states: *"All men are created equal, that they are endowed by their Creator with certain unalienable rights that among these are life, liberty and the pursuit of happiness."* The idea that each member of this country inherently has certain unalienable rights is a founding principle of the country. This idea is a noble one. However, the complete manifestation of this idea requires a certain mindset from the people living in it. First, people as a whole must be a civil group. They cannot be prone to violence when dealing with others who disagree with them. Second, they must be a people who see life objectively in an unbiased manner. Therefore, they would have to be practitioners of self-discipline and restraint. Finally, people should recognize and then reward those among them who are virtuous. This means to reward people who are honest and trustworthy and who treat others the way they would like to be treated. Without this type of mindset, people can be unduly influenced by inconsequential factors such as party affiliation, ethnicity, and social status. Unfortunately, this type of politics is not what is practiced today.

Poli-"tricks" is what is practiced today. A "trick" or trickery occurs when someone believes one thing when the reality is something different. Magicians perform magic "tricks." They make elephants disappear and it appears to be true. However, the reality is that the elephant is still there. Those watching the "trick" just don't realize it.

There are many poli-"tricks" occurring throughout society. A major poli-"trick" in the African-American community of the United States of America is the belief that they must support Democratic candidates exclusively. This was especially true when the first African-American President, Barack Obama was elected. Objectively speaking the question must be asked, "How has the exclusive support of Democratic candidates benefitted the African-American community as a whole?" What is the reality? Although the African-American community makes up approximately 13% of the population, Black men are approximately 50% of the people in jail. The unemployment rate in these communities is typically twice that of the general population. Incidents of police brutality are regularly captured on camera while the officers perpetuating the acts routinely are absolved of responsibility. African-Americans are normally charged more for insurance simply because of where they live. The food is not as fresh as it is in other communities. There's more but I think you get the point.

The only thing that I can see that the African-American community has gotten from this exclusive support is a church visit from candidates during election cycles. For a day or two the chance to listen to political candidates make promises that they rarely fulfill once elected is the greater part of what is received. But other than these occasional visits, little if anything is received in return for this exclusive support. This is poli-"tricks" as the reality of the support is different from the idea.

Another current poli-"trick" comes from those in the majority population who speak of the "greatness" of the United States country. In terms of military superiority, few can argue against this proposition. However in the simple area of being civil to ethnic groups of people, it has not been great. For example, the land of America itself was stolen from both the Native American and Mexican people. The Declaration of Independence did not apply to the African slave although they were human. Asians at one time were forced to work on the railroad in ways similar to that of slaves and many poor whites were slaves to those in control of the land through indentured servitude.

The actual practice of politics by groups of people again requires first that they be a group of people with a mindset of civility towards others and not prone to violence when dealing with those who disagree with them. Next the group needs to be practitioners of self-discipline and restraint as this needed to see life objectively in an unbiased manner. Finally those who are honest and trustworthy should be acknowledged and revered so that their conduct will be emulated by others. This practice is a "Better Way of living life in today's era.

To bring into fruition the actual practice of politics today, study and then emulation of groups that have actually lived in this way should be done. Groups like this can be found all over the world prior to western societal cultural domination and rule. Prior to exposure to Western ideas and systems of thought over the past 2500 years, Africans, Latinos across the Americas, Native Americans, Asians and other groups were traditionally civil in their interactions with others. These groups historically had cultures based upon order, righteousness, justice and truth and routinely revered those of the highest moral character.

By studying these ancient cultures and then adopting those practices today by all, politics can begin to be practiced in a way that was originally intended. A way that will eliminate the numerous "tricks" that have people believe one thing when the reality is different.

Chapter 7

"Male Female Relationships"

Have you ever wanted to have a complete, fulfilling and unconditional type of Love in your relationship with your significant other? So have I. But until recently, I did not know that my current practice of love, a practice I call "Love American Style" prevented me from having this type of male/female relationship.

A significant portion of my life had passed before I realized that my "Love American Style" practice kept me from having the type of Love I wanted. "Love American Style" is calling the satisfaction of wants and needs Love. For example, when I met a woman I was physically attracted to and she satisfied a number of my wants and needs, I thought that these acts were manifestations of Love. Sadly for me, this idea about Love was an unconscious one and I didn't realize that what I was calling Love was nothing more than the satisfaction of my wants and/or needs.

The "Love American Style" practice of love that I engaged in kept me from having a complete, fulfilling and unconditional type of Love. I did not know that this type of Love was NOT Love because of its conditional nature. Love based upon wants and needs like this is conditional because wants and needs change. They never stay the same. The wants and needs I have as a 45 year old man is much different than those I had when I was 15, 25 or 35. These

31

wants and needs are also conditional because they will not be satisfied forever. In my case, the wants and needs that I had grown accustomed to receiving from my mate over time did stop. As a result, over time I thought that my significant other's love for me was subsiding. But I now know that this was not the case. Her cessation of these so called "love acts" did not mean that her Love for me had stopped. It simply meant that as she grew and evolved as a person (which we all do in life) her expressions of Love for me grew and changed as well.

But I did not know any of this at the time. So I held onto my narrow view and wound up becoming a part of the statistics common in those relationships where the "Love American Style" of Love is practiced.

This style of Love is characterized by the following:

1. A 49% divorce rate for first time marriages in the United States; (2006 Edition of Divorce Magazine)
2. A 60% divorce rate for second time marriages in the United States; (2006 Edition of Psychology Today)
3. A desire to have a complete, fulfilling and unconditional type of Love but rarely receiving or giving it;
4. Practicing a form of Love which is limited and conditional.

It was not until I made the following analysis that I began to "see" exactly what I was doing that was preventing me from having what I said I wanted. I asked myself the following:

1. Whose idea was it to practice Love in this kind of way?
2. Where did this idea come from?
3. Did I make a conscious decision to engage in male/female relationships in this way or was the decision made unconsciously as that was all that I knew?
4. Is the "Love American Style" idea about Love true? (Meaning there are no other ways to "practice" Love.)
5. Finally, was this an idea about Love that will stand the test of time?

The objective answering of these questions helped me tremendously. When I engaged in a practice not consciously chosen by me, it should not have been surprising to see that the end result had not been successful for a sustainable relationship.

Many yearn for an unconditional type of Love in their relationships. However I had to find out the hard way that unconditional loving relationships cannot exist in limited Love practicing styles. That's like attempting to place all of the water from the Pacific Ocean into a coffee mug that is in the kitchen cabinet. The water won't fit! We need a different practice, **"A Better Way"** in relationships that will allow us to be able to receive all of the ocean water and more.

Chapter 8

"The Cause of ALL Male/Female Relationship Drama"

In Chapter 7 on Male/Female Relationships I introduced you to a practice in male/female relationships that prevented me from having complete fulfilling and unconditional love in any of my previous relationships. I call this practice Love American Style. This practice equates love with the satisfaction of our wants and needs.

This practice is the cause of ALL present day relationship drama. I now realize that no matter what type of drama troubles a relationship, for example frustration, disappointment, sadness, infidelity, etc., there is only one cause for any of it. Every problem in a relationship at its root is caused by the Love American Style practice.

Consider the following: how does a person feel when he or she does not get the things that that person believes they want or need? They become disappointed. They become upset. Some become sad and even angry. There is a laundry list of adjectives describing people's feelings when things don't go their way. From children to adults, people become upset when they don't get the things they want. The practice of becoming upset when we don't get what we want is common. How upset people become may differ, but all become upset nevertheless.

Now add the following twist to the above. Couples not getting the things each of them want or need have the "strong belief" that a) getting the thing you want will make you happy and b) getting the need satisfied by your mate is what you deserve. What happens then? It intensifies the upset feelings that occur when we do not get what we want. Instead of becoming disappointed, we become <u>very</u> disappointed. Instead of becoming sad or angry, we become <u>very</u> sad or angry.

This is what happens in those relationships where "Love American Style" is practiced. People become so frustrated and sad that they say things they later regret. They do things they later regret. And often, they do things to satisfy their present wants and needs that are not good for the relationship itself. Actions which in that moment they do not regret. An example of this practice is finding other people outside of the relationship who will satisfy these present wants and needs. Hence relationship drama.

I now understand that the "Love American Style" practice for relationships is an IDEA that men and women do not consciously choose. It is an unconscious decision. This practice is all that we know and see. Over time all of us become so accustomed to the practice that we think that this way of being in male/female relationships is normal. Not because it works but because we have not seen any other way. There is nothing normal about continually creating heartache and pain in all of our relationships unless we consider heartache and pain to be normal. To fully accept and implement a "Better Way" in male/female relationships it must be understood that the "Love

American Style" relationship practice creates nothing but heartache and pain.

This practice is the cause of ALL relationship drama. For those who like drama, this is the perfect practice for them. For those who want a "Better Way" that will allow you to have unconditional, complete and fulfilling love with their mate or significant other, read about the solution to Male/Female Relationship drama in the next chapter!

Chapter 9

"The Solution to All Male/Female Relationship Drama"

The typical practice in male/female relationships which I call Love American Style is conditional. It equates love with the satisfaction of our wants and needs. An unconditional practice, "A Better Way" to engage in these relationships is what I believe we all want with our significant other.

To have a complete, fulfilling and unconditional loving relationship, you must remove ALL of the conditions presently in it. Although I like others believed that the satisfaction of my wants, needs and expectations were the cornerstone of my relationships, I now know that these are in fact conditions which led to their demise. Heartache and pain is what I created when my previous relationships were based upon my wants, needs and expectations. I now realize that "A Better Way" of engaging in relationships with our partners happens automatically once these conditions are removed.

There are two parts to "A Better Way" practice in relationships. There is the actual practice itself and the mental mindset necessary to fully implement the practice.

A practical solution is to first recognize that love has nothing to do with what someone does for you. This is not love. It is actually a severe form of egoism. Eradicate this idea. Then, practice not having an expectation that your partner will do anything for you. Accept the following new idea: if my mate does what I want them to do for me wonderful. If they do not, that's wonderful too. Do not rely upon the expectation. Adopt the new idea that if they do what they say that's wonderful but if they don't, something unintentional must have happened which prevented it.

Practice accepting EVERY expression of love from your mate in the same way. Do not minimize or neglect any act. Do not maximize or glorify any specific one or two. If TRUE love is unconditional, why minimize or maximize specific acts and expressions of it? You and your mate deserve to be appreciated for ALL that you do for each other. Not just specific wants and needs.

"A Better Way" (BW) in relationships and "Love American Style" (LAS) have one thing in common. They are both IDEAS about how relationships can be practiced. The major difference is that in the former (BW), you consciously choose to engage in the practice with a clear understanding that it is an IDEA. In the latter (LAS), the IDEA is unconscious so we believe it is REAL. We forget that this is an idea. Our minds become set in this so-called reality and this becomes normal. This view cannot be broken until we remember that the (LAS) practice is not normal or real. Then we are able to choose another IDEA, "A Better Way" with a different practice.

"There Must Be A Better Way of Doing This!"

"A Better Way" in male/female relationships occurs when expectations of wants and needs are eliminated. Relationships like this are free from disappointment, heartache and pain. No one can be disappointed about anything until they first have an expectation that something is supposed to happen a particular way. This new practice eliminates the reasons to be upset. What is left are the many reasons to be content and happy. The feeling I get when I am unexpectedly surprised with unconditional acts and expressions of love is fantastic. Practicing "A Better Way" in relationships allows me to be open to receiving EVERY expression of love by my mate. This simultaneously allows me to be happy for greater periods of time. With continued and sustained practice this new way of being is becoming a new normal for me.

Do not think that "Love American Style" is real and natural. It took time and much practice for this to become our norm. It is my understanding that this is not an IDEA of all people of the world. It is an IDEA most commonly found in Western thinking cultural societies. It is normal not because its practice produces complete and fulfilling male/female relationships. It is normal because western societal thinking nations are the dominate leaders of the world.

They say that doing the same thing over and over again is a sign of insanity. For me, I have tired of being insane in my practice of male/female relationships. So now I am doing something different with a new practice. The something for me is "A much Better Way" of engaging in my relationships. It is working for me. I know it will work for you too! Give it a try.

Chapter 10

"A Resolution for a Happy New Year"

Resolutions are made when we decide on embarking on new beginnings. Often we make resolutions when we have a desire to change something about ourselves. Perhaps we've had a health scare or want to look different for an upcoming event. Resolutions of varying types are made at different times throughout the year. However New Year's Eve is the time of the year when resolutions are consistently made by large numbers of people.

While the typical lose weight, eat healthy, and stop smoking resolutions are typically at the forefront of many people's lists, the following resolution should also be considered for the New Year. Resolve to be "happy" in the upcoming year.

At first glance this type of desire may not seem to be worthy of a resolution. Who doesn't want to be "happy" everyday? However, the type of happiness worthy of a resolution is much different from the type of happiness that many look for presently.

The type of "happiness" worthy of a New Year's resolution is the type that is "perpetual." This type of "happiness" never leaves. It brings with it a continual state of tranquility and peace. It is never moved by conditions or circumstances. Its occurrence is the result of a view of life

41

and practice of how it is to be lived that differs from that which is practiced today. This type of happiness can be contrasted from the intermittent type of "happiness" considered to be normal by people today.

Happiness today is equated with separate individuated pleasant moments. Falling in love, getting a gift, and having fun for example can be thought of as intermittent individuated pleasant moments. These examples have two things in common. First, none of them last. Just as quickly as they come, they go. Second, the intermittent nature of this "so called happiness" produces the opposite of what is longed for. It produces unhappiness. Since individuated moments do not last, desire for the next "happy" moment is created as soon as one ends. Often frustration, being upset and longing for the next "happy" moment occurs. These opposite feelings while one waits for the next happy moment last far longer than the actual moment itself.

The intermittent nature of what is considered as happiness today is anything but that in the African Kamitan Religion of Shetaut Neter. In this tradition, the mental up and down happy one moment and longing for the next moment is considered as "mental agitation." Perpetual happiness is the byproduct of a peaceful and contented mind. This type of mind allows you to experience the higher "spiritual" aspect of yourself. The experience of the "spiritual" aspect of one's Self produces perpetual happiness as this experience allows you to "remember" what you have forgotten. Rekindling of this memory is the purpose of life. It is this experience which gave rise to the term, "Know Thyself."

So the next time you decide to make a resolution, consider a resolution that will change every aspect of your life. Resolve to discover a practice that will allow you to experience a form of happiness free from limitation. This form of happiness is perpetual and not intermittent. A form of happiness that occurs as a result of experiencing the "Self" in the phrase "Know Thyself."

Chapter 11

"The Birth of the S-U-N"

In ancient times prior to the creation of the Judaic, Christian, and Islamic religions, the days leading up to December 25 and those immediately thereafter were considered to be "special." These days were considered as a time for renewal and of giving birth to the divine child in the soul of all. Once born, this child grows and in time leads a person to victory over the forces of ignorance in the personality to discover the peace of self discovery within.

Over time, this period began to be known as the Winter Solstice. The Winter Solstice is a physical representation of a mental and mythological concept representing the birth of the divine child/soul in everyone. This child was metaphorically depicted as the physical "Sun" who was born during this time. In fact, the Winter Solstice period specifically represents the "birth of the Sun" as the Earth goes from experiencing shorter time periods of sunlight. This is referred to as the death of the Sun, the final day of the Winter Solstice to the specific day in which the days begin to get longer. And the birth of the Sun is the first day of the new time period when the days become longer.

In the African Kamitan Religious tradition of Shetaut Neter, this birth was codified into different myths and parables. The most famous one being the myth of Asar, Aset, and Heru. The myth describes the metaphysical

44

process that causes a person to "forget" the divine aspect of their being (soul) and how to give birth to the realization of this divine aspect of the person. It is this birth and renewal of the "Sun" in all of us which allows us to overcome the ignorance that prevents discovery of the deeper regions of the Self within.

As a new year or new period of renewal begins for us all, endeavor to eradicate ignorance so that the mysteries of the soul can be discovered. The underlying mystical wisdom behind this birth and renewal of the Sun opens the way to achieving Enlightenment/Nehast. It is this achievement which the ancestors of Ancient Kamit taught was the purpose of life. As this renewal time period assisted those in ancient times to overcome ignorance and the lower animal nature, consider allowing it to do the same thing for you and all of us in these modern times.

Chapter 12

"Food for the Body, Mind and Spirit"

The present **idea** in society about what is 'proper nutrition' is an obstacle to living a life that will produce complete fulfillment and satisfaction. It is also an obstacle to living a spiritual life. This is true no matter what your particular religious practice is. It is not possible to do either when your body and mind are taking in a variety of poisons and toxins. It is also not possible to understand the subtle aspects of religious and philosophical doctrines in this state. Unhealthy food in the body makes the body work harder to rid itself of materials that do not belong in it. Unhealthy substances prevent your mind from being able to think as it was designed to do. Toxins and poisons create a "cloud" or "veil" over your mind. In this state you can easily fall prey to every whim of the senses. Believe it or not, proper nutrition to all parts of the body helps you find answers to the questions "Who Am I?" and "Why Am I Here?"

BODY, MIND/SENSES, & SOUL COMPLEX

The Body

The body is like a walking/talking conglomeration of the earth. It is the physical aspect of a person that when "enlivened" make up what most of us consider as the total person. Nature has this physical, gross aspect and it is this

46

aspect that you experience through your senses. It exists only in time and space.

The "Spirit"

There is nothing in creation that at its base is not the transcendental essence called "Spirit." Every living thing has it. We know this is so, because it is the absence of this "spirit stuff" which constitutes death. When this "spirit stuff" leaves the body, that person is said to have died. It is this "Spirit" which enlivens the gross elements of creation (the body) and gives what we call life to the natural world. "Spirit" differs from the body because it exists on all planes of consciousness simultaneously.

Additionally, it is this spiritual aspect of you that has the exact same nature of the Divine. The "Spirit" is the higher aspect of a person. It has the same essence as the Divine but in a much smaller degree.

The Mind/Senses

The mind and senses are two aspects that work together to provide balance. You can operate equally between the lower physical realm (the body) and the higher spiritual realm (the spirit) through the use of the mind and senses.

Your senses are designed to experience the lower realm. Everything you can see, feel, taste, touch, and hear all occur in the physical realm. The mind—in fact a purified mind—is needed for you to experience the spiritual aspect of your being.

So the mind/senses allow you to simultaneously experience both the higher and lower realms of existence—but only when fed properly and used properly. Any unbalanced focus on one over the other, leads to a host of problems. An unbalanced focus occurs when one reinforces the **idea** that they are exclusively the "body" only, or that they are exclusively the "Spirit" only.

These are the three aspects of a being which make up the entity known as "you." The body, mind/senses, and spirit ALL have to be nurtured and fed properly. It is these three that grow and mature and evolve through the consumption of a healthy diet. It is also these three aspects that when fed properly and balanced, prepare you to "experience" the higher aspect of your being. This is the nature of the "Spirit."

FOOD FOR THE BODY

Since the turn of the last century, a host of foods eaten by people have been grown using toxins. Many of these same foods before being placed on store shelves contain preservatives to make them last longer. It could be argued that preserving the longevity of a food is a good thing. But what about the side effects associated with the consumption of toxins and preservatives in food?

48

Toxins and preservatives have an effect on the body which is not good. Toxins and preservatives are chemicals that are not natural to the body. They are in fact foreign substances. They are chemicals no different from the chemicals that make up alcohol, cigarettes, cocaine, and other drugs. What do foreign chemicals and substances do in the body? We know that alcohol, cocaine, and other drugs give one a false sense of reality. They skew your perception of what is real and what is not. Is there any reason to believe that the toxins and preservatives in food do not also skew our perception of reality as well?

FOOD FOR THE MIND & SENSES

People are not aware that the mind/sense's "idea of reality" is created through the food that it consumes. People feed this aspect of their being unconsciously. People are often oblivious to the fact that their "idea of reality" is shaped by stimuli over which they exercise no control.

Everything that you interact with through your sense of sight and of sound is food for the mind. Therefore every article or book that you read is food for the mind. Every movie or television show that you see is food for the mind.

Have you ever looked consciously and critically at what you allow to enter your mental space, your mind? Is it good for you? Do the images that come into your mind help you become more peaceful, contented and happy? Or do they create ideas and images that lead to frustration, strife, worry and anxiety? How much thought do you give to what effect all this 'sensory food' has on your mind/senses and how this food shapes your "idea of reality?"

FOOD FOR THE SPIRIT

The "Spirit" also needs to be fed a proper and nutritious diet. Remember that the spirit of a person is that aspect that exists at all times simultaneously on all planes of existence. It is that aspect that gives what is called "life" to the conglomeration of matter known as a body. Once the "spirit" leaves the body, then what is known as death occurs. However death has really not occurred. The body was only 'enlivened' by the "spirit." The body never really was "alive".

Once the "spirit" leaves the body, the "spirit" still exists. "Spirit" does not and cannot die. It is, has been, and always shall be. This is important to realize in reflecting upon proper food for the spiritual aspect of the person.

So feeding of the "spirit" cannot occur through the body. You must **"identify"** with the spiritual aspect of yourself to feed it that which is proper and nutritious for it. To identify with the "spirit" you must transcend the senses. Transcendence of the senses occurs through meditation. Meditation is practicing mental exercises that enable you, over time, to stop the vibrations of the mind due to unwanted thoughts. I recommend that you read the book "Meditation" by Dr. Muata Ashby to explore the process of

50

meditation.

Once your mind is stilled through meditation, you can then "experience" that aspect of yourself that is expansive and complete without limits. This aspect is your "spirit." It is this "experience" that actually feeds your "spirit." The more you feed your "spirit," the more you become one with yourself.

This is proper food for the spirit. Food that lets your spirit "remember" that it is a spirit and not a body.

FOOD FOR THE BODY, MIND & SPIRIT

You are much more than a body that is given approximately 70 years to live. However this is the **idea** that perpetuates society. Every person is born with the ability to recognize the depths of their being right now. Do YOU have an **idea about life** which allows you to recognize the depths of your being right now?

Today begin the process of feeding all aspects of your self properly. Awareness of the underlying essence which gives rise to and supports Creation will occur in a very short time if you do so.

Chapter 13

"Eliminate Emotional Heartache & Pain
In 15 Minutes or Less"

Would you be interested in discovering a way to live life that would free you from emotional heartache and pain forever? Is this information something that would interest you? If I told you that you could learn a technique in fifteen minutes or less that would eliminate both, would you continue reading these words?

You can eliminate emotional heartache, frustration and pain by keeping the following phrase mentally in your mind. "When I Say Up, Me Thinks Down." The phrase again is "When I Say Up, Me Thinks Down."

This simple phrase holds the key to unlocking the cause of emotional heartache and pain. It also contains the solution for its eradication.

To eradicate emotional heartache and pain, we must first understand the method and mode of how our minds operate and function on a second by second basis. This operation is something that few are aware of.

To illustrate how our minds operate consider the following example: if I were to say the word "male" to people not suspecting what I was doing, many of them would immediately think about the word "female." If I were to then say the word "hot," many of those same people would quickly have the word "cold" come to mind. The same thing would hold true if I would later say the word "dark." In this last example, the word "light" is the word that for most would pop into mind. In all of these examples the "opposite" of what was originally thought or considered immediately came to mind. This phenomenon is what I refer to as an "automatic opposite" response operation of our mind.

This "automatic opposite" operation of the mind is very consistent and is always at play. If a person heard another say the word "you", the word "me" in most instances would come to mind. When the word "land" is spoken or heard, a thought or idea about the "sea" or "ocean" is not far behind. This "automatic operation" of the mind is happening every moment with every thought that a person has. This point is important so it bears repeating. This "automatic opposite" response of our mind occurs with every thought that we have. Awareness of how our mind operates in this opposite way is the key to eliminating emotional heartache and pain forever.

So the phrase, "When I Say Up, Me Thinks Down," is a description of how the mind automatically and unconsciously thinks about the opposite of whatever thought exists in the mind at any given moment. The word "I" in the first phrase represents a person having a conscious thought. The word "Me" in the second phrase represents the "opposite" thought that unconsciously comes to mind immediately thereafter.

"There Must Be A Better Way of Doing This!"

It is important to be aware that this "automatic opposite" response of our mind occurs in an unconscious way. Rarely does a person become aware of this process except in those circumstances where he or she is able to separate themselves from the occurrence. For example, this is occurring to you as you are reading these words. The more you read, the more you became conscious of the "opposite" process. However, but for this topic being discussed in this way, conscious awareness of this process would have been elusive.

Now this "automatic opposite" operation of our mind may seem to be a bad thing. Especially given the way it has been presented thus far. It is not. Living a normal and regular life would be difficult at best if this process was not occurring at all times. How would I be able to know the difference between air and a wall if I was unable to immediately be aware of the "opposite" of what I am interacting with? Without the "automatic opposite" operation of my mind at work, I could easily wind up walking into a wall. This could happen because I would have no way of knowing the difference between air and matter.

So I cannot realistically live life without this response system. However, the inability to recognize both that this process is at work every day, minute, and second and how it operates, creates the distress which we refer to as emotional heartache and pain.

"There Must Be A Better Way of Doing This!"

Now you have it. Now you understand how to eliminate emotional heartache and pain forever. "When I Say Up, Me Thinks Down," is the key to this understanding. Now I will place this phrase in the context of practical life situations so that you can see how it operates to create emotional heartache and pain.

Consider the following: everyday people place judgments of value on things in their lives. These things are not inherently good or bad. These things become good or bad based upon the value placed on them. For example a million dollars for one person (me☺) is considered a very good thing. However, this same one million dollars would probably not be as desirable to the Rockefellers, Rothschild's or Fords if they were to lose all of their wealth but for one million dollars. In this scenario they may very well consider this sum to be very bad.

There is nothing inherently good or bad about the one million dollars. What makes it either bad or good is the value judgment placed on having it. In this case value judgment is just like beauty. It resides in the eye of the beholder.

But look at what mentally happens to me when I tell myself that having a million dollars will make me happy. Remember the phrase, "When I Say Up, Me Thinks Down?" As soon as I have the thought, a million dollars will make me happy, the "automatic opposite" operation of my mind kicks in. When it does so, I unconsciously think about its "opposite." By now you probably recognize that its opposite is the lack or absence of one million dollars will make me sad. Now I have given my mind a picture of what **both** happiness and sadness look like in the context of one million dollars.

Unfortunately, what happens to me does not end with a simple mental picture. Now that I have a mental framework of what both happiness and sadness look like in the context of money, "happy and sad" emotions are then placed on stand-by red alert and await the moment to come into being. When I receive a million dollars, I will react based upon my previous notions of what happiness is to me. I may jump up and down, call my family and friends, yell and scream and may go out and party. The happy emotions occur as a result of the "happy" value judgment.

However, the sad emotions will come into existence immediately. They do so because it is doubtful that I will receive this type of money quickly. Now that I have unknowingly equated sadness with NOT having one million dollars, I will immediately begin manifesting these emotions every time the subject of money comes up. I now have an immediate reason to be disappointed, frustrated, sad, upset, disgusted and a host of other "sad" related emotional responses to not having this money. I may even internalize these feelings and may consider my lot in life to be a poor one because of this lack.

The financial example is about an inanimate object. However, the same process occurs when we place value judgments on people or things. As soon as I say that a relationship with this person or getting a car will make me happy, the opposite operation of my mind automatically again tells me what its opposite looks like.

In the context of a relationship, I now know what unhappiness looks like. Now because of what I have done to myself with the value judgment, unhappiness is a forgone conclusion in the relationship. This is because nothing lasts forever. Even if I have the person of my dreams in my life, she is not always going to be the same today as she was yesterday. As she grows and evolves, she will change because nothing stays the same. Additionally, at some point she is going to die.

What's so happy about this state? In the worst case, I now have a present reason to be unhappy because I am not in a relationship. In the best case, I am in a relationship yet still unhappy because my mate is not the same today as she was yesterday.

By now you can see how we are the creators of our emotional pain and heartache. We are the creators of our own frustration. It is self created and self inflicted. It is created because we are not aware of the "When I Say Up, Me Thinks Down" process. Unfortunately the full effect of emotional pain and heartache does not initially appear in its full state. The "sadness" opposite mental picture of "happiness" manifests slowly and expresses itself as a subtle form of longing. This longing over time builds up until it manifests as frustration and discontentment. Frustration and discontentment then grow into a deep form of pain. People hurt and then "feel" it both emotionally and physically.

I submit that discontent is unconsciously experienced by most people. They just don't call it discontent. They call it stress. Discontent is another name for stress. People go to night clubs, concerts and parties to relieve stress. People engage in these activities so they can get a release from all that has happened to them in their life that day or week or month. For an hour or two while at the club, no one has to think about anything! For this brief moment of time, all is forgotten. Even sex today is equated with a stress relief.

But I ask the following: what is it that people don't want to think about? What is it that people want to get away from? What is it that people want stress relief from? EMOTIONAL PAIN, HEARTACHE AND DISCONTENT! People don't want to think because if they do, they will realize how miserable they actually feel. It is the classic case of ignorance is bliss mentality. People are miserable and this is how you can tell.

Do people engaged in activities they enjoy develop stress from doing those activities? Does anyone get stressed out doing things they enjoy? Who wants to forget about the things they enjoy? NOBODY! The only thing that would stop a person from doing what they enjoy is the time to sleep. That's it. So stress and getting away from our daily life routine through escapism like clubs, parties, comedy, etc. is a sure sign of emotional pain and heartache.

"There Must Be A Better Way of Doing This!"

Well the 15 minutes I mentioned at the beginning of this chapter is up. Now you know the origins of emotional heartache and pain. Now you also know that this pain is self inflicted. Therefore, you can today eliminate this from your daily life circumstances. You can do so in this way: from this moment forward, realize that you are the architect of your pain and sorrow by not understanding the opposite operation of the mind. Reduce and then eliminate those things that you place any value judgments on. It does not matter if the judgment is a good one or bad. Eliminate the mind's ability to automatically see an opposite. Keep things totally balanced. What you will get is a mind that is stress free. You will never create frustration or sadness again because you have eliminated its cause. The level of peace that will develop in your life is beyond measure. It trumps any so-called happiness derived from a value judgment.

Chapter 14

"Why Do The Things That Are Fun Make Us Sick?"

Have you ever noticed that the activities that provide people with what they say is the most fun, often result in making them sick?

A friend of mine recently shared with me her enthusiasm for becoming a vegetarian. She had gone about one week without eating any meat. Since I have been a vegetarian for over a decade, I think she believed that I would warmly receive her news and accomplishment. She was correct and I did congratulate her.

In the conversation, she told me that some members of her family had been speaking negatively to her about her new eating habits. In fact, they told her that she needed to have "fun again" and to start eating whatever she wanted. Her response to them was that she didn't think it was fun to eat things that make people sick. It then occurred to me that what's actually sick is the idea that consumption of anything harmful to the body or mind can ever be fun.

At that point I then began thinking about all of the "fun things" that I had previously engaged in. I discovered that many of them literally resulted in making me physically and/or emotionally sick. Thoughts about all of those college days where I drank and had a hangover raced into my head. Back then my friends and I thought drinking and partying was "fun." Being drunk "seemed" fun, but the

60

resulting hangover was not fun at all! For anyone who has ever had a hangover, they know that the impact on the body is a "literal" form of being sick.

I thought about all of the people who smoke or have smoked marijuana. There is little debate that marijuana destroys brain cells. For those in their teenage or young adult years, this type of destruction causes an injury to the development of the brain.

And then one day I said to myself, whose brilliant idea was it that called all of this stuff FUN? It wasn't me! I never made a conscious decision to adopt a belief system like this. I did this because this was I all that I knew. Even when I was stretched out by the toilet vomiting after drinking all night wondering why I was doing this to myself, the next day I was right back to drinking. But this was "fun" to me because this is all that I knew "fun" to be while growing up. This is what I saw the older people do when I was a kid. This is what my friends and I snuck around and did when we were not old enough to do it legitimately.

And then I asked myself the same question again. "Whose brilliant idea was it that called all of this stuff fun?" Again it wasn't me." Who was it?

Was it someone who has had 2 or 3 heart bypass surgeries because it was "fun" to eat a lot of fried greasy food and a lot of red meat?

Was it someone with throat or lung cancer because of the "fun" one has by smoking cigarettes?

Was it someone with high blood pressure due to the stress inherent in the "fun" activities of chasing, screwing and impregnating as many women as one can?

No, I doubt that it was any of their ideas. Whose brilliant idea then was this?

The answer to this question is one I am still searching for. Until this answer is discovered, consider a new idea about "fun." One that I will now share with you which I have implemented into my life. From this day forward resolve that your idea about "fun" things will only be comprised of things which will give you more life and give it to you more abundantly. "Fun" things will consist only of those things that make your body, mind and spirit become more healthy and vibrant. "Fun" things will consist only of interactions that make your family and male/female relationships complete and fulfilling.

Therefore adopt a new idea about society's current definition of "fun." Stop considering activities that harm your body, mind or spirit "fun." Begin considering these activities to be something to be refrained from doing. For example, endeavor to consider the present societal definition of "fun" as something unhealthy, makes you sick, and is not good for you at all! Eating and drinking whatever one wants, as an example, when it makes the body sick is barbaric. These are some examples of how you can change your thinking in this way.

Eating well, speaking well, and doing unto others as you would have others do unto you, can and should be the "real" barometer of what "fun" actually is. Do you see why the present idea about "fun" is sick?

Conclusion

As a result of reading each of the chapters and taking the time to reflect on the content, my thoughts are that there definitely is a "better way of doing these things."

Remember to continue to look at the various challenges in your life and ask yourself:

1. What is the current idea "driving" my current practice or way of acting?

2. Where did this idea come from?

3. Did I accept this idea unconsciously or adopt it consciously?

4. Is the idea true?

5. Is it an idea that will stand the test of time?

These key questions can help you attain a better way of living life and definitely living it more abundantly.

Peace and Blessings on your Journey to a "**Better Way**" of doing this!"

PRODUCTS BY THE AUTHOR

"YOU!

ARE RESPONSIBLE FOR YOUR LIFE!

"*You*, **Are Responsible For Your Life!**" is a modern day book of philosophy for the 21st century that provides "practical" advice to assist the reader in living life more spiritually. The person who wants to know the answer to the question, "Who Am I." It is a must read for those people of today who believe that "we are spiritual beings having a human experience." It is also a must read for the person who wants to take Complete control over every aspect of their personality.

Ultimately the book is about our ***IDEAS.*** What
they are. What they are not. How they color and influence
our perception of reality. An influence which often keeps
us stuck in decades old behavior patterns that prevent us
from having the type of life we say we want. A life of
<u>perpetual</u> joy, peace and happiness.

ISBN: 0978634608
Cost: $15.99

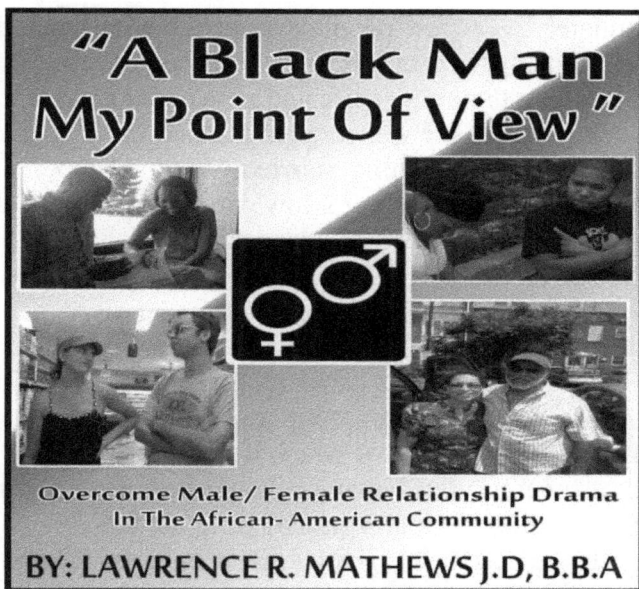

"A BLACK MAN, MY POINT OF VIEW"

OVERCOME MALE/FEMALE RELATIONSHIP DRAMA IN THE AFRICAN-AMERICAN COMMUNITY.

"A Black Man, My Point of View," was written to help couples achieve what many say they want. A relationship that fulfills their dreams and desires.

"There Must Be A Better Way of Doing This!"

Unfortunately, very few people ever achieve this state in their relationship. In fact it is more common than not that a person can live their entire life and never achieve one relationship like this. Even couples married for 25+ years in many cases are unhappily married. What is happening in our community that does not allow couples to achieve the state that many yearn for?

People do not realize that the foundation of relationship drama is formed at the beginning when relationships start. In fact, I assert that the demise of a relationship is certain based upon that foundation. It is not a matter of if. It is a matter of when. Relationship drama unfolds as unconscious behavior patterns direct and impel a person to act in ways that negatively impact the relationship. These patterns are known as "drivers" and are revealed. Solutions are provided to overcome them.

ISBN: 0978634616
Cost: $13.99

"There Must Be A Better Way of Doing This!"

A NOTE ABOUT THE AUTHOR

LAWRENCE R. MATHEWS HELPS PEOPLE LIVE WELL!

LAWRENCE R. MATHEWS, J.D., B.B.A., DRAWS ON HIS PROFESSIONAL AND PERSONAL EXPERIENCES TO ALLOW OTHERS TO VIEW LIFE AS FULL OF OPPORTUNITIES. HE TRANSLATES COMPLEX PHILOSOPHIES INTO PRACTICAL STEPS FOR CREATING A LIFE FULL OF JOY AND ABUNDANCE.

HIS DIVERSE BACKGROUND INCLUDES A BACHELOR'S

DEGREE IN BUSINESS ADMINISTRATION AND TEACHING IN BOTH THE DETROIT, MICHIGAN AND GLENDALE, ARIZONA SCHOOL SYSTEMS. THE FIRST IN HIS IMMEDIATE FAMILY TO GRADUATE FROM COLLEGE, HE THEN EARNED HIS LAW DEGREE PRACTICING AS A TRIAL ATTORNEY. AS AN ATTORNEY HE HAS PRACTICED BEFORE THE MICHIGAN SUPREME COURT.

HE IS A BUSINESSMAN, MOTIVATIONAL SPEAKER, AUTHOR OF SEVERAL ARTICLES AND THE FOLLOWING BOOKS:

1. "15 QUESTIONS TEENS WOULD LIKE TO ASK THEIR PARENTS BUT DON'T"

2. "YOU ARE RESPONSIBLE FOR YOUR LIFE!"

3. "A BLACK MAN, MY POINT OF VIEW ON IMPROVING MALE/FEMALE RELATIONSHIPS"

4. "GUIDE TO PRACTICING THE EGYPTIAN MYSTERIES."

LAWRENCE'S AFRICAN KAMITIC NAME MEANS "OPENER OF THE WAY" AND HE USES THE WISDOM OF ANCIENT PHILOSOPHIES AND RELIGION AS A GUIDE TO FRESH INSIGHTS FOR HIMSELF AND OTHERS. HE IS A PRACTITIONER OF EGYPTIAN YOGA, MEDITATION AND VEGETARIANISM ALONG WITH BEING A FATHER AND GRANDFATHER.

"There Must Be A Better Way of Doing This!"

www.ingramcontent.com/pod-product-compliance
Lightning Source LLC
Chambersburg PA
CBHW021912040426
42447CB00007B/818

9 780978 634643